The Secrets Hidden Within

Mary Alexander

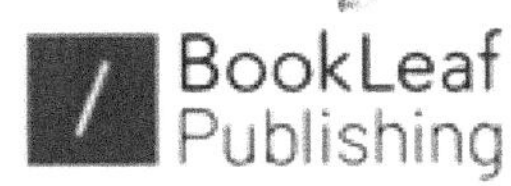

BookLeaf Publishing

Presentation by *BookLeaf Publishing*

Web: www.bookleafpub.com

E-mail: info@bookleafpub.com

ISBN: 9789357210591

First edition 2022

DEDICATION

I would like to dedicate this book to the three people who love me in this world. To my mother, Forsyth, I owe everything I have and everything I've done, to you. To my sister, Anna, who has ferociously stood by my side, when it seemed as if no one else in the world would. And to my boyfriend, Kane, who continues to lift me up, continues to push me to be the best version of myself I can be. Thank you.

Snow

Winter's grace fools everyone
Into believing that it is cruel and unkind
But the snow that dances
Along your fingertips or eyelashes
Isn't so harsh

Or how the sun shines in between
The trees that are frozen and bare
Making the most dazzling colors
or lack there of
As if diamonds are in the place
Of the leaves that now are gone

Maybe you've even noticed
After the chills have settled in the air
Just how forgiving the wind can be

For once you've stepped inside
And the cold has thawed itself from your lips
You'll find a loved one or two

And next to the fireplace you'll sit
Drinking in in the warmth
That only two seasons ago
You protested against

But your happiness is what winter wants most
Which is shown by the blankets of snow
If you're lucky enough to receive them

For with these blankets come joy and laughter
From those both young and old
As snowballs soar through the air
or ice skates shoved on the smallest feet

And those smiles given in secret
As you recall just how many times
Winter has taken you by surprise
With all the beauty it produces

Time

Someone once told me
That the only constant
Is change
But what about time?

It slips through our fingers
Every second different from the last
Every second trying its hardest
To be different
To be noticed
To being better than the previous one

But seconds always lead
Into minutes
The minutes courageously
Changing into hours
And even when something so drastic
So life-changing happens
Time still continues
Not one minute skipped
Not one second passed by

Time continues on
Even when nothing else does
And I guess without time
There is no change

Secrets

You ask me for a secret
Something only I keep
Something that no one else knows
But I don't think you'd like my answer

I've kept so many secrets from you
Tightly tucked away behind my heart
So that no one could touch them
Or take them from me
Not even you

Because I've always been nervous
Letting you see the inside of me
The way your mind makes me melt
As I slip away into your thoughts

Or how my dreams are filled
Of only getting your attention
To the point where I do not wish to wake up
For leaving the dream world, leaving you
It's not something I ever want to do

The Sun

Why do you think you admire
The sun more than the moon?
The moon, you think, is beautiful
Flawed but still shinning

She is calm and kind
She listens
She's almost everything
You could ever ask for

But what about the sun?
Do you not see how much he loves her?
Do you not admire him for his undying love?

He says, "touch her and I'll burn you"
He's unmerciful to everyone
But the moon?
Well, he spares no one but her

And oh how she lights up because of him
How he dies to let her live
They aren't destined to be together
And yet they love

The one true tragedy
For both the sun and the moon
Is how they are star-crossed

Love Like a Poet

I love like a poet
I'm selfish as the sea and sky
I absorb your pain until it is mine

And I flood cities with tears that I have no right
to
I squeeze your hands so tightly
Your knuckles pop

Because I see
Old couples at sunset
With linked arms
And I want to crush peace into you

I brush my thumbs beneath your eyes
Trying to wipe away the purple shadows
And I leave ink stains on your face.

In the end

What if in the end
We realize that our lives
Were never about points on the line

Or the dates on the calendar
Or markings on the walls
That life was never about
The food we did or didn't eat

Or the days we missed our alarm
Slept an extra hour
Or missed our ride.

What if we realize that goodbye
May actually mean goodbye.
And that it was never about the ending at all.

Only you can see

So for what it's worth
I lay my heart before you once again
As you step unheeding
Along a road that only you can see

This is the way I am
The only way I know
Even as I accept
That my everything will fall just short
I'll never measure up
But I'll keep trying still.

I know I shouldn't need to hear you tell me
But without the acceptance
I'm wandering on a path
With no significant end

You've built me up
Kindled a flame within me
That now struggles to stay alive
Yet you shun my attempts
To give back what you gave
I need to know you need me too

When we go our separate ways

Will you walk away
With the part of me I offer

Or will you continue along that road
That only you can see
Heedless of the impact
of the flame that still needs tending
and of my self-doubt
I cannot do this alone

Unopened Windows

Gone are their words
Bound between the covers of forgotten books
There they lie, undisturbed
Hardly inviting the passer-by to look

Were their feelings of no worth
Hearts borne to pages now left to the dust
Fated to be buried as their bodies in the earth
Lost to memories as corrupt as rust

Oh modern man, searching his soul
Seeking to understand what seems unknown
Have you ever turned to man of old?
Is it not out of him you've grown?

How different can the two be?
Old and new, man seeks his bliss
This has eternally been man's dream
Looking to be inspired by heaven's kiss

Open these windows to those lost in time
Words left by an ever expressed heart
Etched in pages left by the seemingly divine

From the souls that now transcend eternity sublime

Bittersweet

Bittersweet
Are my favorite days
Because I know the feeling never lasts

In between islands of paradise
Icy ocean surely do lie
Following the current of life
In my rickety raft

Each island holds parts I need
To turn this raft into a yacht
Sooner or later
My schooner will be complete
Waiting for my lady
To board my masterpiece

Someday my heart will lead me
To the one I seek
Its completing piece

Until then I will not rest
Building and mapping
Through feelings and mist
Hoping to find a heart's bliss

Thick Skin

She speaks
Choking on her own hardened tone
Didn't mean for it to come out that way
She wants revenge
But who would know?

Lackadaisical she appears
With her woven scarves
That smooth her frayed silhouette
And skirts fashioned of patchwork quilts
That billow in the wind
When she dances to the songs
Of restless trees

Her gaze is soft
and the tunes she hums are sweet
as her fingers graze the strings
of an antique mandolin.
Melodies of summer she sings,
and I reminisce about lazy days and
how we used to lick our fingers of melted honey
paste
as we lay in the orchard by the side of the farm,
sometimes after dusk.
But I recall that something happened one night

after we parted,
and by dawn the pears were frothy
and plums were clad in wool overcoats.

Interrupted are the whispers of the past,
for now as I see her glow in the sunset
and listen to each timid pluck of the strings,
I hear only discord
and a distant plea,
and my tongue turns sour.

She wants revenge
but they wouldn't know,
they wouldn't ever know,
because she is

oh so terribly sorry,
I didn't mean for it to come out that way.
Please forgive me.

Able to decieve, she is,
as am I able to
scrub her clean with my eyes
and peel back her skin.
She refuses to mend,
so I tear her apart
by each delicate seam
in hopes that she will someday feel something
harsher than a broken string.

So that for once,
as she flies across the fields
like a fool,
her cream-thick skin will be burned by the
winds.

Imagine

Imagine if we dared to envision love
Like a universe
In its wholeness

I would let my gaze wander
Looking Into your eyes
For as long as I want
I would let my body
Feel into your beautiful energies

Imagine if I was to enter
Your whole heart
And I owned it

With a selfish yet selfless greed
With a dominating yet pure hold
While I draw all your affections
From every feature of your face

As I stare at you endlessly
And hold your hands
Until you know nothing of coldness in life.

The Sidewalk

The time and place remind me
Of an old country singer
It is a rare occasion
For me to be awake
At this time of day

My eyes are still blurry
My mind wandering the scape
As if it were a candy store

I notice all the warm colors
As I embrace the music around me
And observe the vividity
Of the ground, trees, and sky

Notice the difference
Between the light of home
Versus the light
Of this new terrain

I then climb to a venue
To greet the light
And feel the chill of its power.
It renders me with humility
As I embrace my own breath.

The river of life

Is this what life is?
A robotic stroll
Through random events

No one thinks
No one seeks perspective
Or even truth

They seem to already know it
By shutting it out
They think that whatever it is
Doesn't concern them

Just a puppet
Who never admits to strings

Or maybe I am who sees what isn't there
A mind making its own hell
Analyzing the flow of life
Have I forgotten how to swim?

My thoughts weigh me to the bottom
Watching the people flow by
Only noticed by some

The depth it goes
Breeds illusions of thought
Can peace be brought?

The final act

The movement of your eyes
Betrays fear to me
Yet for you
There is no reason to panic

The movement of your lips
Describes to me the anxiety
In this small little era
This curious epoch

The soft sigh whistles
Through the small smile
The very idea of your memory
Is not enough forever

But this is the final act
Of the reality for so long we shared
It takes no visible effort
To swirl around and walk away

Yet your feet
They were like
The heaviest regrets

As you flow into the dark distance

And fade forever
The memory speaks to me
in the language of a defunct land

Your book of life

Once you've been there
You carry the place forever in your heart
Slip into the aroma of your lullaby scent
The fragrance coloring the air
That carries you far beyond

It's the scent from a thousand years ago
You will remember what your eyes see
So what does your undying mind picture?
when the sweetly dangerous
Or forbiddingly beautiful scent
Returns to your spirit?

In our dreams, we see different paths
And old places once roamed
There's a sea of faces and a blur of strangers
Vague voices whisper secrets of your past role
For your old heart

When the sun dust dies for star shine
You are a sleeping baby, the releasing souls
Into heroic, cowardly, frightening, bemusing
Odd and magical dreams
Make sure to pay close attention
For these dream lights depict your true story

Nothing will ever be learned
In one chapter of your life
Do you even know
What was the first word to your beginning?
Dare not skip ahead
And pry into your book of life

The book is infinite.
Lifetimes fly, flow and pass
And you will never complete the book
Because it is your souls ancient history
And electric, mesmerizing, future

We are shaping the story
Delicately writing the chapters
and building our plots
Be careful what masks you create
And keep an eye on who your villain is
becoming
Because his darkness is yours
And his redemption depends on you alone

Curious sparks in the wind
We flitter away chaotically like dragonflies
Seeking to live life after life
Demanding walks and dances
Along life's glowing rose gardens
and dead wastelands
With new shoes, new skin, and the same old soul

It's just gossip

I know I'm not perfect
I know that I have had my fair share
Of helping drama get spread
Of even helping drama start

But that's the thing
I understand this
I apologize
When I've done something wrong
And the only people I will talk about it with
Are those that I can trust

Those that I know won't spread it around
Because they, like me
Know what damage they could do
If they did
And they don't want to do it

They don't want to hurt the people
That might get hurt
Because they value that friendship
And that's the main problem with people lately

They don't value others

They're only in it for themselves
And so what if they hurt someone else
Because of some juicy gossip that they heard on
the street?
It's just gossip, right?

I don't want to be cinderella

In honesty?
I've never cared much
For the story of Cinderella

Not for the fact
That the stepmother was horrid to her
Not for the fact
That the stepsisters did any way possible
To get Cinderella into trouble

And not even for the fact
That her father was completely out of the picture
Due to her stepmother

It's the fact
That the prince continuously chases her
Not knowing whether or not
Cinderella actually wants to be found

He does this on his own accord
Without taking her thoughts into consideration
And I find this unacceptable
Especially in this day and age

What if she didn't want to be rescued?

What if she felt she could handle herself on her
own
Breaking free of her stepmother's rule
And finding a way to live on her own?

Her fairy-godmother certainly helped
With the dress and carriage
And getting to the ball on time
Maybe she could help her out in breaking free,
too?

But the prince didn't consider this
He only went after her for selfish reasons
Because he wanted her, so he believed that she
wanted him, too.
Just because she left her glass slipper behind
Didn't mean she needed to be rescued

Story of a crush

It's a terribly tragic story
About a girl who had a friend
Many years ago
That was just a friend

And it wasn't until
She started dating her boyfriend
That she realized
She actually had feelings for this friend
But their friendship had fallen apart

Several years pass
With this friendship beginning and ending
Over and over
In a horrible circle
Because he's apparently obsessed
With making her miserable

And she's the imbecile
Who keeps letting him
Because she likes to believe the best in people
Despite being shown otherwise

They stopped talking for a couple of years

And she began to believe that their circle had
finally broken,
When lo and behold he comes back

And now
Now that she is finally single
And has had a horrible year
Decides to reach out

And the only thing standing
Between her finally telling him
Her feelings for him

Is the fact that now
He is the one in a relationship
And for once, he is happy
And she doesn't want to ruin it

In too deep

I can get so scared
Of what I begin to feel
I'm glad that we don't talk
As often as I would like

Because it would make
These quiet times harder
or at least harder than they already are

Because now I've seen his body language
Now I've seen his mannerisms
Now I've seen how he is around other people

And it just makes this so much harder for me
Because now I can put words with the person
Ehen before all I could do was see words
And I feel as if I'm just in too deep.

How much you've won

I will never understand
Why give me your number
If just a few days later
You plan on never talking to me again?

I know the signs
Because it's how it always plays out
I wanted to rush it this time
Since I just can't set myself up
For more heartbreak with you

And I told you that
I told you how vulnerable I am right now
I told you that I don't need you screwing me
over again
I told you to just get whatever you were
planning over with

It's not as if you can use
Anything against me now
Since everything's already out in the open
But you don't know that
Because I refuse to let you know how much
you've won

I can always move on

I've always been timid
When it comes to telling someone
How I truly feel about them
In the positive sense

Negatively, I have no problems
With telling others what I actually feel
Without a regard to their feelings at all

But telling someone
How I feel about them
Even if they're just a friend?
It scares me to death

I've never understood why
What's the worst that can happen
They tell me they don't like me anymore?
They tell me they don't return my feelings?

I can always move on
I can always find someone else
Who'll return my feelings
Yes?